A Young Citizen's Guide to News Literacy

OPINION VS. NEWS

Danielle Haynes

PowerKiDS press

New York

Published in 2019 by The Rosen Publishing Group, Inc.
29 East 21st Street, New York, NY 10010

First Edition

Editor: Jill Keppeler
Book Design: Reann Nye

Photo Credits: Cover, p. 27 GaudiLab/Shutterstock.com; p. 5 Vasily Smirnov/Shutterstock.com; p. 7 tdoes/Shutterstock.com; p. 9 Buncha Lim/Shutterstock.com; p. 11 Sean Thomforde/Shutterstock.com; p. 13 Toronto Star Archives/Toronto Star/Getty Images; p. 14 Syda Productions/Shutterstock.com; p. 15 Iakov Filimonov/Shutterstock.com; p. 17 ESB Professional/Shutterstock.com; p. 19 Sopotnicki/Shutterstock.com; p. 21 Allkindza/iStock Unreleased/Getty Images; p. 22 Andrey_ Popov/Shutterstock.com; p. 23 Pressmaster/Shutterstock.com; p. 25 Tashi-Delek/E+/Getty Images; p. 28 Westend61/Getty Images; p. 29 archana bhartia/Shutterstock.com; p. 30 Jose Luis Pelaez Inc/Blend Images/Getty Images.

Cataloging-in-Publication Data

Names: Haynes, Danielle.
Title: Opinion vs. news / Danielle Haynes.
Description: New York : PowerKids Press, 2019. | Series: A young citizen's guide to news literacy | Includes glossary and index.
Identifiers: ISBN 9781538346129 (pbk.) | ISBN 9781538345009 (library bound) | ISBN 9781538346136 (6 pack)
Subjects: LCSH: Media literacy—Juvenile literature. | Journalism—Juvenile literature. | Mass media—Objectivity—Juvenile literature.
Classification: LCC P96.M4 H377 2019 | DDC 302.23—dc23

Manufactured in the United States of America

CPSIA Compliance Information: Batch #CWPK19: For Further Information contact Rosen Publishing, New York, New York at 1-800-237-9932

CONTENTS

CRACKING THE CODE

As you flip through a newspaper, look at a news website, or even click through the channels on the TV, you'll come across lots of different kinds of information. Some of it will be factual, but some may be based on the opinions of the person who wrote the article or presented the broadcast. To be an informed citizen, it's important for you to be able to tell the difference between news and opinion in the media—and it's not always easy!

Sometimes writers, editors, or broadcasters will give readers clear labels to show if something is news or opinion. Other times, you'll have to look for clues. There are different words that can tip readers or viewers off. Being a good consumer of the news means being able to quickly understand this code.

BREAKING NEWS

"News literacy" is, in part, the ability to understand and judge news reports. People with good news literacy should be able to tell the difference between a news report and an opinion piece.

People are faced with dozens of examples of journalism each day. It's important to be able to tell the difference between a report meant to inform and one that's meant to change your mind about a topic.

NEWS, NEWS EVERYWHERE

You can get news in many different places. As **technology** changes, **journalists** find new ways to spread information. Sometimes there is overlap—newspapers and cable news channels may also have websites, for instance.

<u>Print</u>—information shared on paper
• newspapers
• magazines
• newsletters

<u>Broadcast</u>—information shared over the airwaves
• television news
• radio news

<u>Internet</u>—information shared on a website or app
• news websites
• blogs
• podcasts
• social media

SECTIONS OF A NEWSPAPER

In nearly every newspaper and on every news website, there are many different types of stories or articles. Similar types of articles are grouped together so readers know what kinds of stories they can expect to see in certain places. News stories are usually on the same pages (print or web) as other news stories. Those pages, together, are called a section.

Most major news organizations also have opinion, sports, and features sections. The sports section has stories about athletic events or athletes, such as your favorite NFL team's games or a local high school's track stars. Features sections—sometimes called lifestyles sections—can include stories about interesting people, arts or entertainment events, restaurants, or other topics. Bigger newspapers, such as the *New York Times*, will have more specific sections with stories about health or travel.

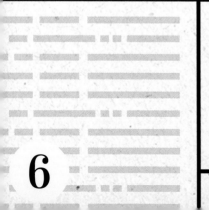

BREAKING NEWS

News outlets usually feature news stories before anything else, but sometimes other stories lead, or go first. If a local sports team wins a championship, it may appear on the front page or at the top of a news website because it's a big story that lots of people care about.

Bigger newspapers may include more sections on topics such as business and fashion. However, papers in smaller towns may have a community section to run local birth announcements or information on things such as church dinners—things larger city newspapers may not cover.

Style

SPORTS

METRO

BUSINESS

TODAY
YOUR LOC
NEW

"I think we're
that big
on Li

WHAT IS NEWS?

Unsurprisingly, news outlets focus on news stories. These stories are based on facts and answer six important questions: who, what, when, where, why, and how. The main purpose of a news article or broadcast story is to inform readers about something that has happened or will happen.

Journalists often write news articles in what's called the "inverted pyramid"—or an upside-down triangle. This means the biggest, most important information goes at the top of the story. Less important facts go later, more or less in order of importance. Stories are organized this way in part so if editors need to cut a story quickly, they can cut sentences from the bottom. Sometimes articles on websites will be longer because space isn't as much of an issue.

BREAKING NEWS

News articles should contain facts, or information that can be proven to be true. Opinions, however, are personal beliefs, which not everyone will agree with. They should also be based on fact, however.

Good news stories start with a first sentence—or lede—that should answer as many of the "five W and H" questions as possible. Later paragraphs will include supporting information and quotes from people the writer interviews.

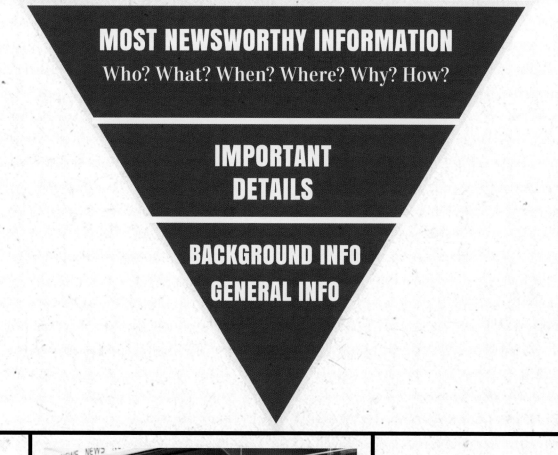

MOST NEWSWORTHY INFORMATION
Who? What? When? Where? Why? How?

**IMPORTANT
DETAILS**

**BACKGROUND INFO
GENERAL INFO**

TYPES OF NEWS

Articles in the news section and news broadcasts are sometimes referred to as hard news or straight news. This is because they're more serious in nature than, say, the features section or sports news.

Take a look through the news pages of your local newspaper or its website. You'll notice different kinds of stories even within this one section. They may be separated by geography—international, national, state, or local. The *Washington Post*, one of the biggest newspapers in the United States, has an entire section **dedicated** just to world news.

There are also different topics. For example, crime and courts stories follow criminal acts, such as robbery or assault, and then charges and trials for the suspects. Political stories are about government meetings, laws, or elections.

BREAKING NEWS

Investigative journalism also produces news articles. These may be a series of articles in which reporters dig up facts about **unethical** or criminal acts, such as a company illegally polluting the air and trying to hide it.

Sometimes reporters cover **disasters**, such as fires, earthquakes, or storms. Some disasters affect a few people, while others affect thousands or even millions.

WHAT IS OPINION?

Opinion pieces are a different type of journalism. The writers of these pieces are trying to convey an opinion and influence how you think about a topic.

Newspaper readers can find most opinion pieces on an editorial page or specific opinion section. There may be an op-ed page in your local newspaper. "Op-ed" stands for "opposite editorial." It's called that because it may be located on the page opposite or next to the editorial page.

Opinion pieces are often personal in nature. The writer may tell readers how they believe the readers should vote or whether the readers should support a new law. They may point out a problem they see in the world. Some opinion pieces can be found outside the opinion section. Reviews of concerts and movies may appear in a features or entertainment section.

Opinion pages sometimes include editorial cartoons. These are drawings that show the artist's feelings about a topic. Editorial cartoons may be funny or may be serious—or both. This cartoon honors firefighters who fought wildfires in Canada, comparing them to superheroes:

TYPES OF OPINION

In the opinion section of a newspaper or website, you may see editorials, columns, and letters to the editor.

Editorials don't have a byline, or a line with the author's name, because they represent the views of the newspaper as a whole. Many newspapers have editorial boards. An editorial board is a group of editors who decide what opinion to take on an issue, such as what candidate to support for political office.

Columns usually include a small photo of the writer. They may be regular features and run once a week or so. Some columns have themes. One writer might like to write about politics, while another might write about community issues such as road conditions. Readers write letters to the editor to share their own opinions.

Have you read something on a news website or in a newspaper that you agree or disagree with? Try writing a letter and maybe your opinion will be published, too!

PICK UP A PEN!

Anyone can write a letter to the editor. Here are some tips to getting your letter printed in a newspaper or published on a website:

• Keep it short and get to the point early.

• Use words that show opinion, but remember to include facts to back your opinion up.

• Don't forget a call to action! For example, if you think the city council should vote for a new park, make sure to tell them.

WORDS MATTER

Another way to tell the difference between a news story and an opinion piece is by looking at the words the writer uses. News stories are supposed to be objective, which means they include only facts, not the writer's opinions. Opinion pieces are more subjective, which means writers use words to describe their own feelings and view.

A news reporter might describe a suspect in a robbery as a 6-foot-tall man with brown hair and blue eyes—facts that can be proven. But the reporter should never write that the man looked mean or grumpy.

Why does this matter? Well, what if the man is innocent? If the reporter used words showing a **negative** opinion to describe the suspect, the public might unfairly think he's guilty.

Think of ways to objectively describe this person and ways to subjectively describe this person. Would the words you choose be different if you knew who she was? If you were a news reporter, they shouldn't be!

SUBJECTIVE OR OBJECTIVE? TEST YOURSELF!

Try writing down some words to describe your best friend. Can you think of a way to describe your friend objectively? If you write down that someone is 10 years old and has curly hair, those would be facts. You can prove them. Can you think of a way to subjectively describe your friend? You could say they have pretty eyes or stinky feet. Those are your opinions, but maybe someone else thinks your friend's feet smell delightful!

17

The only time a news reporter should use words showing opinion in an article is when they're quoting someone that watchers or readers can **presume** to have necessary knowledge about something. For example, if the police are looking for a robbery suspect, they might say he's "armed and dangerous."

An opinion writer is free to use more subjective words to try to make a case for why readers should agree with their viewpoint. The more strongly a writer feels about a topic, the stronger their language will be.

Opinion writers also can refer to themselves using the word "I" since they're talking about personal viewpoints. For example, a columnist might write, "I believe the sidewalks on Main Street should be replaced because they are ugly and dangerous."

BREAKING NEWS

When reporters give their opinion in a news piece, that's called editorializing. Editorializing may cause a reader to question whether writers are changing the facts of a story because they have strong opinions on the subject.

Reporters must be careful about the words they use. Even something as simple as describing a five-story building as "large" is subjective because someone from a city with much bigger buildings might consider that five-story building to be small.

SPOTTING THE DIFFERENCE

Other than word choices, what are some ways you can tell what's an opinion piece or news story? Readers may find opinion pieces in almost every section of a newspaper or news website. Movie reviews may go in the entertainment section. Sportswriters pen columns for the sports section. Opinion pieces should be clearly labeled as opinion. However, even if they're not, sometimes the people who design websites or newspapers also give readers clues.

Opinion piece headlines often have different styles of lettering compared to news headlines. In print, the **text** of an opinion piece may be ragged along the right side, while a news article's text is often flush, or straight on all sides. Columns often include a small photograph of the writer.

Sometimes opinion headlines or newspaper names use serif fonts. This means the letters have little "feet" at the end. News headlines may use sans serif fonts—those without the feet.

LET'S TALK ABOUT FONTS!

Fonts are the style of lettering a newspaper, book, magazine, or website uses. Some are plain. Some are fancy. Some look a little silly! Newspaper designers often use different fonts for opinion piece headlines than they use for news headlines. This can help readers identify which is which. Opinion headlines may be italicized, which means the letters lean to the right. *Like this*. However, sometimes features stories and big news stories may have headlines in different fonts altogether.

IDENTIFYING OPINION ONLINE

It can be harder to tell the difference between opinion and news on news websites and in social media posts like those on Twitter and Facebook. The homepage of many news websites will include links to various sections, including news, sports, and opinion. There may even be an area on the homepage listing opinion articles. But since a website isn't designed quite like a newspaper, there won't always be the same clues for opinion pieces.

Try looking for a label. Labels such as "column," "**analysis**," "editorial," "commentary," "essay," "viewpoint," or "**perspective**" means there will be some opinion in a piece. If you're still not sure, check to see if the writer uses subjective or objective language. Most subjective language (outside quotes) will be in opinion pieces.

It's important to pay careful attention to what you read online, because not all news organizations will make it clear if an article is news or opinion. Use the skills you've learned to figure it out for yourself!

NEWS ON SOCIAL MEDIA

Do you use Facebook or Twitter? How about Instagram? If so, you probably see people sharing many articles. If you only look at the headlines—often the only thing you can see on a social media post—you're not getting the full story. And it might be harder to tell news from opinion because you can't see what section of the news site it's filed under. Pay attention!

TELEVISION NEWS

Television news (cable and local) uses its own set of clues to help viewers tell the difference between facts and opinions. Pay attention to how people are described during a news program. An anchor is the person who hosts a show or news broadcast. In news programs, anchors usually give only facts. Correspondents are reporters who have gathered facts about a story and will discuss them with the anchor. Commentators give their opinions on topics. They're like newspaper or website columnists.

Analysts and contributors give expert information on topics. Their statements may contain opinion. A police expert, for instance, may **speculate** about why she thinks someone committed a crime before police can tell the public all the facts of the case.

BREAKING NEWS

If you're still not sure if someone's expressing opinion or reporting news, listen for personal statements. If the speakers refer to themselves with the word "I," then it's probably an opinion.

Even though they usually report only the facts, some TV news anchors will give their opinions. As a good news consumer, it's important to listen for when anchors use editorializing or subjective language.

TAKING SIDES

Local TV news programs usually stick to just reporting the news. However, cable TV news stations include both news and opinion because they must fill a lot more time each day—24 hours! Commentators are journalists, and they have the responsibilities of journalists. However, cable TV news programs may also host people called consultants, pollsters, or **strategists**. They're not journalists! They're sometimes paid to represent a side. Pay attention to how programs identify people.

BIAS IN THE NEWS

Although news reporters are supposed to just stick to facts, sometimes opinion can sneak into a news story in the form of **bias**. Bias happens in a news story when reporters let their personal point of view affect the way they write an article or present a story.

Even a whole news organization can have bias. This may be based on political leanings. If a newspaper favors the current president, employees may tend to write articles that make the leader look good. On the other hand, news organizations that disagree with the president may publish more critical articles about the leader.

Biased news articles may be based in fact, but they give readers only part of the information. Well-informed readers should get their news from many different news organizations so they can see multiple perspectives.

BREAKING NEWS

Opinions can't be wrong, but they can be based on information that is wrong. Opinions should be based on real facts.

Some people may think a news organization is biased if it reports things they don't like or agree with. This may be true—but it isn't always! Look for the facts before making up your mind.

27

WHY IT MATTERS

Now that you've learned some ways to spot the difference between news and opinions, you can put your new skills to use. But why does it matter?

While some columns and editorials contain the same elements as news articles, such as facts about current events, they're often one-sided. If you only get your information from the opinion pages of a newspaper, you won't always get the full story. A columnist trying to persuade people to vote for a mayoral candidate may leave out the politician's bad behavior, for instance.

On the other hand, an opinion writer can inspire readers to look at a topic a new way. A letter to the editor could persuade readers that plans for a new shopping market could spoil the peace and quiet of a neighborhood.

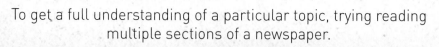
To get a full understanding of a particular topic, trying reading multiple sections of a newspaper.

29

GO FORTH AND LEARN!

With so many sources of news out there today—including newspapers, radio, television, and the Internet—it's more important than ever to be smart about where you're getting your information. Unfortunately, you can't trust that every news organization will clearly tell you what is news and what is opinion. Sometimes you must do the work yourself.

Remember to look for the visual clues! Does it say "world news" or "editorial" at the top of the page? Does the article headline say "analysis" above it, and is there a photo of the author? What kinds of words does the writer use—subjective or objective?

Now that you're armed with some of the tools you need to be an informed citizen, go out and read and listen to as many news sources as possible so you can get the facts and learn what other people think about them!

GLOSSARY

analysis: A careful study or explanation of something.

bias: A tendency to believe that some people or ideas are better than others.

dedicate: To decide that something will be used for a certain purpose.

disaster: Something that happens suddenly and causes much suffering and loss for many people.

journalist: Someone who works with the collecting, writing, and editing of news stories for newspapers, magazines, websites, television, or radio.

negative: About the real or supposed bad qualities of something or someone.

perspective: Point of view.

presume: To logically think that something is true.

speculate: To think about something and make guesses about it.

strategist: Someone who uses strategy or a plan of action to achieve a goal.

technology: A method that uses science to solve problems and the tools used to solve those problems.

text: The words that make up a book, website, or another piece of writing.

unethical: Not following ethics, or rules based on what's right and what's wrong.

31

INDEX

WEBSITES

Due to the changing nature of Internet links, PowerKids Press has developed an online list of websites related to the subject of this book. This site is updated regularly. Please use this link to access the list: www.powerkidslinks.com/newslit/opinion